These windows bring a smile to your heart every time you look into the eyes of your loved ones. Enlarge your photos to 8" x 10" so you can really see the faces. Feather butterflies add just the right embellishment on this creative canvas.

Windows to the Soul

by Michelle Tornay

MATERIALS:
- One 24" x 24" Canvas - *Canvas Concepts*
- Paint (White, Baby Blue) - *Making Memories*
- ½" x ½" wood strips (One 20" long, Two 11" long)
- ½" x 1½" wood strips (One 21" long, Two 22" long)
- One 24" long crown molding
- Feather butterflies - *Country Market*
- Transparencies - *Hewlett-Packard*
- Adhesive (Scrappy Glue) - *Magic Scraps*
- White finishing nails, silk flowers, staple gun

INSTRUCTIONS:
1. Cut crown molding and wood pieces to fit the canvas. Paint all of the wood pieces White. Let dry.
2. Paint the canvas Baby Blue. Let dry.
3. Nail crown molding in place from the back of the canvas.
4. Nail the outer frame wood pieces in place from the back. Glue small wood pieces in place, starting with the vertical piece, then adding the horizontal pieces. Turn the canvas over and staple from the back, through the canvas.
5. Place the transparencies as desired.
6. Mount an 8 x 10 inch photo in each square .
7. Glue butterflies and silk flowers in place.

Fancy iron corners.

Pretty Pink flowers.

When photos capture inner beauty so perfectly, don't hide them in a scrapbook. Make a captivating canvas that will enhance any room and give you joy every day!

Beauty Lives Within

by Michelle Tornay

MATERIALS:
- 12" x 24" (or 2-12" x 12") Canvas - *Canvas Concepts*
- Paint (Parchment, Rose Pink) - *Plaid* Folk Art
- Patterned paper - *Chatterbox*
- Cardstock - *Bazzill*
- Ink - *Nick Bantock*
- Silk flowers
- Iron corners - *Provo Craft*
- Canvas words - *Li'l Davis*
- Ribbon - *Offray*
- Conchos - *Scrapworks*
- Adhesive (Tape) - *3L*
- Adhesive (Scrappy Glue) - *Magic Scraps*

INSTRUCTIONS:
1. Paint the entire canvas Rose Pink. Paint the iron corners Parchment. Brush the sides of the canvas lightly with Parchment paint.
2. Glue the iron corners to the 2 upper corners of the canvas.
3. Cut a 12" x 12" sheet of patterned paper in half. Adhere halves to the bottom half of the canvas.
4. Cut a 12" x 12" sheet of Flower print in half. Turn it over. Tape the pieces together. Tear and ink the top of the paper.
5. Cut the canvas words into 3 separate words and sew them in place.
6. Adhere the Flower print to the solid paper.
7. Glue 4 flowers in place.
8. Place 4 conchos evenly along the ribbon. Attach the ribbon to the bottom of the canvas.
9. Cut 3 cardstock mats 4¼" x 6¼". Ink the edges. Sew 4" x 6" photos to the mats.
10. Tape matted photos in place.

Long before kindergarten, you became friends. You still strive to stay in touch, even though you live on different coasts. You've seen each other through job changes, marriages, and pregnancies. You call each other once a week just to find out how the kids are doing. This artwork honors a bond that goes beyond friendship.

FOREVER FRIEND

by Krista Fernandez

MATERIALS:
- One 12" x 12" Canvas - *Canvas Concepts*
- Nutmeg Brown paint - *Plaid*
- Cardstock (Pink, Rose) - *Bazzill*
- Alphabet rubber stamps - *Barnes and Noble*
- Button Alphabet rubber stamps, Rhinestones - *PSX*
- Chocolate Brown ink pad - *Rubber Stampede*
- Lilac embossing powder - *StampnStuff*
- Embossing ink pad - *Tsukineko* Versamark
- Die-cut metal letters - *JoAnne Scrap Essentials*
- Aluminum - *Art Emboss*
- Lavender mesh - *Magic Mesh*
- Purple check ribbon - *Offray*
- Colored staples *Work.org*
- Adhesive (Tape) - *3L*
- Adhesive (Glue Dots)
- Fiber, bead trim, sponge paint roller

INSTRUCTIONS:
1. Paint canvas using a sponge roller and Nutmeg Brown paint.
2. Ink the edges of an 8½" x 11" Pink cardstock with Brown. Adhere to the canvas.
3. Adhere a strip of shiny Purple paper 4½" x 12" to canvas.
4. Adhere beaded trim to the bottom edge of the Purple paper.
5. Tear a piece of Rose cardstock for the mat. Moisten the edges and curl with fingers.
6. String fiber on the top of the Purple cardstock. Staple fiber to the edges.
7. Adhere photo over the string.
8. Photo corners: Punch a square out of aluminum and then cut in half diagonally. Dip corners in a Versamark ink pad and cover with Lilac embossing powder. Heat. Repeat 3 times. Adhere rhinestones. Attach to the photo.
9. "4 ever" Tag: Freehand cut a small tag and add magic mesh. Thread ribbon through the metal eyelet "4" and glue to tag. Stamp "ever" on a scrap of Rose cardstock and adhere to tag. Set eyelet in tag. Thread fiber through eyelet and tie.
10. "Friend" tag: Freehand cut a larger tag from Pink cardstock and ink edges with Brown. Adhere metal letters and add fibers. Tie ribbon to tag.
11. Stamp initials on squares of Lavender cardstock. Adhere in place.
12. Add a strip of ribbon and rhinestones.

Great corner treatments.

Fabulous beads and glitter.

Perfect transparencies.

There is no doubt about how this artist feels about her daughter. Hang this project in her room, or in the family room as a wonderful, positive statement of love. The colors and composition in this project blend with "absolute perfection". Display your favorite photo in a charming setting with papers and embellishments that complement the subject.

Absolute Perfection

by Suzy West

MATERIALS:
- One 14" x 14" Canvas - *Canvas Concepts*
- One 8" x 10" wood plaque
- Paint (Pink, Blue)
- Patterned paper - *Chatterbox*
- Ribbons - *Li'l Davis*
- Flower petals, Metal photo corners - *Making Memories*
- Heart Rhinestone stickers - *PSX*
- Beaded ribbon, transparency sheet

INSTRUCTIONS:
1. Paint the canvas and plaque. Let dry.
2. Adhere pattern paper to the canvas.
3. Adhere photo to plaque. Attach plaque to the canvas.
4. With your finger, add paint to the edges of paper to blend with canvas.
5. Adhere beaded ribbon to the canvas below the paper.
6. Wrap ribbon around the plaque.
7. Print and adhere the transparency sheet to the canvas.
8. Add painted photo corners to the canvas and the photo.
9. Add the flower petals to the canvas and place rhinestones on them.
10. Add extra rhinestones to the canvas as desired.

november 8 1999
1134 am
7LBS 10 OZ

JorDan D MagpOc

JULY 13 2003
1 12 PM
6LBS 15 OZ

Jasmin D MagpOc

Precious hands cast in metal.

Attach sweet little favors.

Celebrate the joy of twins with this sweet set, or make a canvas for each grandchild. Also makes a great gift for the grandparents.

Our Bundles of Joy

by Emelyn Magpoc

MATERIALS:
- Two 12 x 12 inch Canvases - *Canvas Concepts*
- Acrylic paint (Blue, Pink, White) - *Making Memories*
- Mod Podge, Crackle Medium - *Plaid*
- Patterned paper - *PSX Designs*
- Brown ink pad - *Nick Bantock*
- Glaze pen - *Sakura* Gelly Roll
- Frames - *Ikea*
- Metal memorabilia - *Li'l Davis*
- Metal corners - *Michael's* Card Connection
- Ribbon, Ribbon words - *Making Memories*
- Ribbon - *Offray*
- Letter stickers - *me & my Big ideas*
- Adhesive (Diamond Glaze) - *JudiKins*
- Adhesive (Glue Dots)
- Baptism favor, candle

INSTRUCTIONS:
For Blue canvas:
1. Paint canvas with 2 coats of Blue paint. Let dry.
2. Tear patterned paper diagonally. Crumple patterned paper and flatten it out. Mix White paint with water to thin it. Paint patterned paper to soften the pattern. Let dry. Distress the paper by inking randomly. Attach paper to canvas.
3. Adhere metal corners with Diamond Glaze. Use letter stickers for journaling information. Adhere Ribbon Word to canvas.
4. Coat the entire canvas with Mod Podge to seal the paint.
5. See instructions for frame.
6. Attach candle, and baptism favor to canvas.
For frame:
Apply 1 coat of paint to frame. Let dry. Apply 1 coat of crackle medium. Let dry. Apply 1 coat of White paint. Ink frame edges. Attach Ribbon word along the bottom of the frame. Tie ribbons to frame. Attach Metal Memorabilia to the top of the frame. Insert photo into frame. Use a glaze pen to add color to the frame. Adhere frame to canvas.
For Pink canvas:
Follow above directions, but mirror image and use a Pink color scheme.

Turn your canvas into a bamboo raft and let your imagination sail away to your favorite vacation spot. With its seashells and flowers, this delightful trio will brighten any room.

ALOHA

by Krista Fernandez

MATERIALS:
- One 12" x 12" and two 6" x 6" Canvases - *Canvas Concepts*
- Creamy Peach paint - *Plaid* Apple Barrel
- Dark Orange cardstock - *Bazzill*
- Orange cardstock - *National*
- Coasters - *Market Bazaar*
- Eyelet flowers, Orange mini snaps - *Making Memories*
- Ribbon - *Garden Gate Designs*
- Classic lettering stencils - *C Thru 1*
- Bamboo place mat, mini snaps, jute, vintage buttons, seashells

INSTRUCTIONS:
1. Paint all canvases Peach. Let them dry.
2. Large canvas: Cut a piece of Orange cardstock 8½" x 12". Adhere it to the top of the 12" x 12" canvas.
3. Glue the Blue ribbon to the bottom of the Orange cardstock. Add vintage flower buttons.
4. Wrap jute around 2 corners of a 5½" x 8" photo. Mount photo on Dark Orange cardstock. Tear, moisten and curl the edges of the cardstock. Adhere to the canvas.
5. Stencil the title on Dark Orange cardstock with Peach paint. Cut out a rectangle around each letter. Add mini snaps. Adhere to the canvas.
6. Bamboo frame: Cut apart a bamboo place mat. Overlap the corners and tie with jute. Adhere to canvas.
7. Randomly glue seashells to the bottom of the canvas.
8. Small canvases: Cut two 3¾"squares and two 5¼" squares of Dark Orange cardstock.
9. Glue photos to the small mats. Glue the large mats to the canvases.
10. Thread a ribbon through the top of each coaster. Glue a matted photo to each coaster.
11. Wrap jute around a corner of each coaster. Attach a metal flower accent. Glue coasters to canvases. Glue seashells at each corner of the canvas.

Bring at least one multi-generational photo out of the album with this canvas. This is an opportunity to create a memory for your children, and share the names and stories about these relatives.

Family Ties

by Emelyn Magpoc

MATERIALS:
- One 14" x 14" Canvas - *Canvas Concepts*
- Mod Podge - *Plaid*
- Acrylic paint (Brown, Pink) - *Making Memories*
- Patterned paper, Embossed Vellum - *K&Company*
- Patterned paper - *Mustard Moon*
- Letter stamps - *Ma Vinci*
- Brown ink pad- *Nick Bantock*
- Black ink pad- *Tsukineko* StazOn
- Pink ink pad - *ColorBox* Cat's Eye Chalk Ink
- Wooden letters - *Li'l Davis*
- Ceramic tiles - *Accentology.com*
- Ribbon - *Offray*
- Trim - *Decorative Details*
- Adhesive (Diamond Glaze) - *JudiKins*
- Wooden knobs

INSTRUCTIONS:
1. Paint canvas with 2 coats of Brown paint. Let dry.
2. Cover canvas with light patterned papers. Ink the edges with Brown.
3. Cut another patterned paper 11" x 12" Adhere to canvas.
4. Cut embossed vellum 8" x 12". Ink embossed area to emphasize patterns. Attach embossed vellum to patterned papers.
5. Coat the entire canvas with Mod Podge to seal the paint and papers.
6. Adhere photo. Adhere decorative trim around photo and the lower part of the canvas where the patterned papers meet. Add color to the trim with Pink ink.
7. Paint the wooden knobs Brown. Apply Pink ink. Seal with Mod Podge. Adhere knobs above the trim. Tie bows above the knobs with tails long enough to reach bottom of the letters.
8. Paint the ceramic tiles with Pink acrylic paint. Ink edges and surface of tiles with Brown. Stamp "TIES" with Black ink. Coat the tiles with Mod Podge to seal. Adhere tiles over the ribbon tails.
9. Paint the letters "Family" Pink. Adhere in place with Diamond Glaze.

Add textures for dimension.

Nautical wheels add whimsy.

Ships Ahoy! My daughter loves sailing, boats, docks and water. She has a collection of toy boats. I took these photos down at the boatyard, and her expressions were so delightful, I made this canvas to hang in her room.

Little Sailor

by Suzy West

MATERIALS:
- Two 14" x 14" Canvases - *Canvas Concepts*
- Red paint - *Making Memories*
- Pattern paper - *Mustard Moon*
- Blue cardstock - *Bazzill* Basics
- Stamps - *Making Memories*
- Brown ink pad - *Nick Bantock*
- Wood tiles - *EK Success*
- Seashells, 2 wood ship wheels
- Adhesive (Scrappy Glue) - *Magic Scraps*
- Adhesive (double-sided tape)
- Burlap netting, moss, rope, cardboard, transparency sheets, staple gun

INSTRUCTIONS:
1. Staple canvases together in the back, front, and ends.
2. Paint the canvas Red. Let dry.
3. Tear, crinkle and ink the edges of the paper. Center paper on canvas and adhere.
4. Staple burlap netting all over the canvas.
5. Glue the three pieces of wood together for the corner. Wrap wood several times with rope. Glue wood to canvas.
6. Stamp "Little Sailor" onto the transparency sheet.
7. Mat large photo on Blue cardstock. Glue in place.
8. For dimensional effect, 1 small photo is not attached to the canvas. Back that photo with cardboard to stiffen it. Then tape it to the loose crinkled paper on the upper right corner of the canvas.
9. Glue 2 small photos to the lower left corner of the canvas.
10. Glue wood letter tiles, moss, seashells and wood wheels in place.

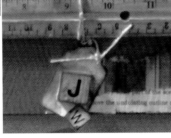

Fun tile letters paired with a dressed up book plate.

A collaged tag teamed with a wooden ruler adds interest.

Recently, my son fulfilled a life-long dream to become an astronomer with NASA. Looking back, he had always been the inquisitive one in the family. He has always wanted to find new ways to solve old problems. This canvas says a lot about how he became who he is.

THINK BIG THOUGHTS

by Suzy West

MATERIALS:
- One 12" x 24" (or 2-12" x 12") Canvas - *Canvas Concepts*
- Acrylic paint (Red, Blue)
- Mod Podge - *Plaid*
- Patterned paper – *7gypsies*
- Patterned paper – *Mustard Moon*
- Brown ink pad
- Wood letter tiles, Book plate, Number stickers, Label - *Li'l Davis*
- Adhesive (Scrappy Glue) - *Magic Scraps*
- Adhesive (double-sided tape)
- Tag, burlap, jute, ruler, transparency, stencils, staple gun

INSTRUCTIONS:
1. Paint the canvas. Let dry.
2. Adhere large photo with double-sided tape.
3. Print title on transparency sheet and adhere over photo.
4. Tear, crinkle, and ink pattern paper.
5. Glue patterned papers and small photo on the left side of the canvas.
6. Paint the words using stencils and acrylic paints.
7. Staple the burlap to the canvas. Glue paper, book-plate, and label in place.
8. Glue wood letters in place. Add number stickers.
9. Ruler tag: Ink tag. Glue wood letters to tag. Add a piece of jute. Wrap jute around ruler. Glue ruler in place.
10. Seal entire canvas with Mod Podge.

"Well behaved women rarely make history."
When I was little, Aunt June was my favorite
aunt. She was so vibrant. She was always doing
interesting things. So, I was absolutely ecstatic
when I found these old photos of her in a box in
Mom's attic. This canvas is in her memory.

Intriguing canvas letters -
tops!

Vintage buttons and lace add
to the old fashioned theme.

Remembering June

by Krista Fernandez

MATERIALS:

- 12" x 24" (or 2-12" x 12") Canvas - *Canvas Concepts*
- Patterned paper (Red diamonds, Red cardstock, Green stripe) - *Chatterbox*
- Patterned paper (Isabella Floral Printed Embossed paper) - *K&Company*
- Chocolate Brown ink pad - *Rubber Stampede*
- Canvas alphabet letters - *Carolee's Creations*
- 2 safety pins – *Making Memories*
- 1 heart shaped clip - *Making Memories*
- Adhesive (Scrappy Glue) - *Magic Scraps*
- 3 Nails, vintage lace, gingham fabric, walnut ink, vintage buttons

INSTRUCTIONS:

1. Stain canvas with walnut ink.
2. Cut a 2½" x 12" strip of Floral paper. Glue strip to left side of canvas.
3. Cut Green stripe paper 5½" x 9½". Glue it to the lower right hand corner of the canvas.
4. Cut Floral paper 9" x 9½". Glue to canvas.
5. Mat photo on Red cardstock. Glue to embossed paper.
6. Print "remembering" on Red cardstock. Tear and ink sides with Chocolate Brown. Glue canvas letters in place. Cut 2 small strips of Gingham fabric. Attach safety pins to fabric and glue to title block. Glue title block to canvas.
7. Mat photo on Green stripe paper. Glue to canvas. Adhere a small strip of Gingham fabric, buttons, and heart clip to the corner.
8. Attach a strip of vintage lace to the bottom of the canvas. Wrap lace ends around the canvas and staple to the back.
9. Cut 2 strips of Red diamond paper ¾" x 9" and ¾" x 5". Glue in place. Add buttons.
10. Cut 3 diamonds from diamond paper. Moisten, crumple and flatten. Glue to canvas.
11. Hammer in 3 nails along the right side of the canvas. Tear 3 strips of Gingham fabric and tie around nails.

Our families are very important to us. That is why we hang portraits on the walls and make heritage scrapbook albums. This creative canvas gives you another way to adorn a wall while conveying that vital message: "this is who we are". This artwork helps us connect with loved ones, especially those who live far away. When you make your canvas, choose embellishments and papers to match the personality of your family.

Luscious leaves from the vine to accent.

Racanelli

by Suzy West

MATERIALS:
- One 12" x 24" (or 2-12" x 12") Canvas - *Canvas Concepts*
- Burgundy paint
- Pattern paper - *K&Company*
- Pattern paper - *7gypsies*
- Pattern paper - *Carolee's Creations*
- Copper embossing powders - *Suze Weinberg*
- Metal photo corners - *Making Memories*
- Wood plaques (One 8" x 10"h, two 5" x 7")
- Adhesive (glue)
- Transparency sheet, vine/grapes, staple gun

INSTRUCTIONS:
1. Paint the canvas and the plaques Burgundy. Let dry.
2. Tear pieces of different pattern papers. Adhere to the canvas.
3. Glue plaques to the canvas.
4. Adhere torn paper to the 5" x 7" plaques.
5. Adhere photos to the plaques.
6. Print family name on a transparency sheet and glue to a small plaque.
7. Emboss metal corners with Copper.
8. Add embossed photo corners to the photo and title block.
9. Wrap vine around the top and right hand side of the canvas. Staple in place.
10. Glue extra leaves from vines to the canvas.

It's time to take all the photos and notes off the refrigerator door and give them a permanent home on this easy to assemble ribbon board. Painted tin lids are perfect magnet boards, and the ribbons allow you to change your photos whenever you want.

RIBBON BOARD

by Emelyn Magpoc

MATERIALS:
- One 12" x 24" (or 2-12" x 12") Canvas - *Canvas Concepts*
- Acrylic paint (Brown, Navy, Pink)
- Mod Podge - *Plaid*
- Patterned paper - *PSX Designs*
- Cork - *Creative Impressions*
- Printed Mounts - *Design Originals*
- Tag, Buttons, Circular clip, Nickel buckle, Angel wings, Playing card - *Scraps-n-More.com*
- Eyelet heart, Rub-On, Ribbon word - *Making Memories*
- Metal letters - *K&Company*
- Ribbon - *Offray*
- Adhesive (Diamond Glaze) - *JudiKins*
- Adhesive (Glue dots)
- Flowers, metal tins, binder clip, decorative beads, magnets

INSTRUCTIONS:
1. Paint canvas with 2 coats of Brown paint. Let dry.
2. Apply ribbon to the patterned paper. Tape ribbon ends to the back of the paper. Adhere flowers and beads to ribbon intersections. Attach assembly to the left side of canvas.
3. Adhere cork to the canvas. Add buttons as shown in photo. Add ribbon word through the nickel buckle on the right side of the canvas as shown.
4. Slide photos under ribbons. Arrange flowers in small mount. Adhere leaf/heart decoration to painted tag. Add handmade painted heart to center of angel wings. Attach binder clip to cork border and clip playing card to it. Attach circular clip to ribbon.
5. Drill holes in metal tins. Paint tins with 2 coats of Navy. Let dry.
6. Apply Rub-On to the top tin. Coat the tins with Mod Podge to seal.
7. Place tins on the canvas to determine where to poke holes in the canvas. Run ribbon through the holes to attach metal tins. Tie in place. Attach notes and memorabilia with magnets to metal tins.
8. Add photo behind printed mount. Add ribbon and metal letters. Adhere to canvas.

Love like this does not happen every day. Cherish it and display it with an artistically themed collage that coordinates so well with the sepia tones in the photograph. Any nostalgic photo would work well in this setting, especially old wedding photos.

Love Beyond Measure

by Suzy West

MATERIALS:
- One 14" x 14" Canvas - *Canvas Concepts*
- Plum paint
- Pattern paper - *Chatterbox*
- Cardstock - *Bazzill*
- Brown ink pad - *Nick Bantock*
- Sticker ruler - *EK Success*
- Tile letters - *Westrim*
- Letter stickers - *me & my Big ideas*
- Metal letter, Buttons, Clips - *Making Memories*
- Key charm - *Once Upon A Charm*
- Adhesive (Tape) - *3L*
- Wood ruler, ribbons, safety pin, burlap, jute, 60" tape measure

INSTRUCTIONS:
1. Paint the canvas Plum. Let it dry.
2. Tear and ink the edges of 2 coordinating papers. Tape torn papers to the striped paper. Adhere burlap.
3. Wrap ribbon around the paper, taping ribbon ends to the back.
4. Tie jute and charm around wood ruler. Glue in place.
5. Add photo.
6. Create your title with embellishments.
7. Add ruler sticker and buttons.
8. Sand down everything but the photo.
9. Glue tape measure around the outer edge of the canvas.

1. Paint canvas Red. Let dry. Apply 1 coat of Mod Podge.

2. Trim lattice strips to make a frame around the canvas. Paint frame and shelf wood Black. Let dry. Coat with Mod Podge.

3. Cover the top 18" of canvas with chicken wire. Secure with staples.

4. Attach Black frame with nails.

5 Adhere shelf to canvas using Liquid Nails. Attach decorative corners under the shelf with nails and Liquid nails.

6. Screw in decorative knobs by hand.

7. Stamp "family" onto cardstock and cut out in shapes of tags. Attach to the chicken wire using ribbon and brads.

8. Embellish clothespins as desired. Clip photos to chicken wire.

9. Apply "Love" Rub-On to Black cardstock. Cut out a tag shape. Clip to photo.

10. Emboss "together" in Black on mount. Wrap Red ribbons around mount and knot. Tie a charm to one of the ribbons. Tape photo into printed mount. Clip to chicken wire.

11. Emboss daisy in Silver on Black cardstock. Cut out a square. Clip to chicken wire.

12. Thread Gold ribbon through the side of the frame.

13. Use spiral clips to attach notes to the chicken wire.

14. Glue styrofoam into the bottom of the tin bucket. Add silk flowers and excelsior. Adhere tin to the shelf.

If your style is more "country", this project will really appeal to you. Chicken wire provides many places to clip photos, tags, and memorabilia. The shelf is a good place for keys, and the knobs are handy for hats.

Family

by Krista Fernandez

MATERIALS:
- One 24" x 24" Canvas - *Canvas Concepts*
- Paint (Black, Barn Red) - *Making Memories*
- Mod Podge - *Plaid*
- Cardstock (Manila, Black)
- "Love" White Rub-Ons, Alphabet stamps - *Making Memories*
- Maggies Daisy stamp - *Stampendous* Perfectly Clear
- Pixie alphabet stamp, Heart button - *PSX*
- Black ink pad - *Hero Arts*
- Red ink pad - *Nick Bantock*
- Embossing powder (Black, Silver) - *StampnStuff*
- Spiral clips - *Creative Impressions*
- Brads (Heart, Yellow) - *JoAnne Scrap Essentials*
- Printed mount - *Design Originals*
- Iron decorative corners, Decorative knobs - *Provo Craft*
- Ribbon (Black and White gingham, Red, Red sheer, Gold) - *Offray*
- Tin box - *Mainstays Crafts*
- 1½" wide lattice strips (Two 15¾" long, Two 24" long)
- 4" x 24" lattice strip for shelf
- Adhesive (Liquid Nails) - *Macco*
- Adhesive (Glue Dots)
- Chicken wire, charm, buttons, silk flowers, excelsior, styrofoam, calendar page, clothespins, staple gun, nails

Delicate daisies in the garden

A picket fence sets the scene.

These photos of Sierra are so bright and happy, I painted the canvas to show the sunshine she brings into our lives. This art takes me into the yard with her every time I see it. I hope the canvas you make brings you the same joy.

NATURE'S GIFT

by Suzy West

MATERIALS:
- Two 14" x 14" Canvases - *Canvas Concepts*
- Paint (Yellow, White, Tan) - *Delta*
- Crackly Medium - *Plaid*
- Cardstock (Pink, Green) - *Bazzill* Basics
- Moss - *Luster Leaf Products*
- Adhesive (foam tape, glue)
- Fences, flowers, cardboard, staples, staple gun, transparency

INSTRUCTIONS:
1. Staple canvases together with a staple gun. Staple in the back, front, and ends to help secure the canvases.
2. Paint the canvases and fence. Let dry.
3. Cut cardboard in the shape of an awning. Paint it Tan. Let it dry. Paint crackle on the awning. Let dry. Paint the awning once more. Let dry. Glue awning to top of canvas.
4. Adhere fence to canvas with foam tape. Glue moss to the bottom of the fence and top of the awning. Add flowers all over.
5. Mount photo on cardstock. Adhere photos to canvas.
6. Print title on a transparency. Adhere to canvas.

Wise words of wisdom to impart.

Ashley has the happiest countenance. I love her expressive eyes. I like this simple layout because it focuses attention on her sweet expressions. The colors were chosen to complement her bedroom decor.

Be Yourself

by Krista Fernandez

MATERIALS:

- Two 12" x 12" (or 1-12" x 24") Canvases - *Canvas Concepts*
- Stoneware Gray paint - *Creative Touch*
- Paint (Old Ivy, Green) - *Plaid*
- Mod Podge - *Plaid*
- Cardstock - *Bazzill*
- Black marker - *Zig* Writer
- Wood flowers - *Paper Craft*
- Metal label holders - *Making Memories*
- Letter stickers (Tiny type, Tiny trinkets) - *Paper Fever*
- Ribbon - *Offray*
- Staple gun
- Adhesive (glue)

INSTRUCTIONS:

1. Staple canvases together.
2. Cover the right side of the canvas with Light Green cardstock.
3. Mat larger photo on medium Green cardstock and then onto a larger, darker Green mat.
4. Use letter stickers to spell out "ashley" and cover with label holder. Attach using mini snaps. Handwrite "yourself" in lower right corner.
5. Paint the letters B and E with Stoneware Gray. Let dry. Coat with Mod Podge for a glossy finish. Adhere to the large Green mat.
6. Cut 3 shades of Green cardstock strips 4" x 12"
7. Adhere all 3 side by side to the left side of the canvas.
8. Paint 3 wooden flowers in coordinating colors. Coat with Mod Podge for a glossy finish. Adhere to canvas.
9. Mount 2 smaller photos to the left side.
10. Create "sweet" and "happy" with small letter stickers and attach to canvas. Glue label holders over the words. Glue mini snaps in place.
11. Trim the outside edges of the canvas with gingham ribbon.

Nap Time says the clock.

Great letters spell a message.

Nap time allows children to dream away the afternoon. Preserve those peaceful moments to make into memories.

Dreams

by Michelle Tornay

MATERIALS:

• Two 12" x 12" (or 2-12" x 24") Canvases - *Canvas Concepts*
• Baby Blue paint - *Plaid Folk Art*
• Patterned paper - *Carolee's Creations*
• Cardstock (Tan, Blue) - *Bazzill*
• Brown ink pad - *Nick Bantock*
• Clock hands - *Limited Edition*
• Metal letters - *K&Company*
• Label stickers - *Pebbles Real Life*
• Adhesive (Tape) - *3L*
• Adhesive (Scrappy Glue) - *Magic Scraps*
• Adhesive (photo corners)
• Wood letter, clock face, staple gun

INSTRUCTIONS:

1. Paint both canvases and the large letter with Baby Blue. Let dry.
2. Staple the canvases together side by side.
3. Cut the following cardstock pieces: Tan: 4½" x 4½", 1¼" x 4½", 7½" x 7¾"; Blue: 1¾" x 7½", 4½" x 7¼". Ink all the edges with Brown.
4. Tape cardstock to the canvas as shown in photo.
5. Ink the edges of the patterned paper and tape it in place.
6. Use the photo corners and tape to mount the photo in the center of the patterned paper.
7. Glue the clock face in place. Glue the clock hands in the desired position.
8. Ink the edges of the large letter. Glue it in place.
9. Glue the metal letters to the upper left side of the canvas.
10. Mount the stickers and letters on the Blue cardstock on the bottom right side of the canvas.

Fantastic wood, die-cuts and rub-on letters announce the place.

Layer your creation.
Canvas • Plaque • Photo

Textured burlap and lovely shells add interest.

Create the perfect escape for any room in your home with this absolutely gorgeous presentation. If you haven't been lucky enough to travel to an exotic destination, gather pictures from travel agencies and the internet to make your getaway canvas.

KAUAI

by Michelle Tornay

MATERIALS:
- One 12" x 36" (or 3-12" x 12") Canvas - *Canvas Concepts*
- Paint (Baby Blue, Linen)
- Manila cardstock - *Bazzill*
- Brown ink pad – *Nick Bantock*
- Shells - *U.S. Shells, Inc.*
- Simply Stated Rub-Ons - *Making Memories*
- Hawaii Die cut - *Deluxe Die Cuts*
- Wooden letters - *Li'l Davis*
- Adhesive (Scrappy Glue) - *Magic Scraps*
- Adhesive (Tape) - *3L*
- 7 x 9 inch wooden plaque, burlap, staple gun

INSTRUCTIONS:
1. Paint the entire canvas Baby Blue. Let dry. Ink the edges.
2. Paint the plaque Linen. Let dry. Ink the edges.
3. Pull the burlap around each side of the canvas and staple it in place.
4. Glue assorted shells to each side of the burlap.
5. Cut 4 Manila mats 4¼" x 6¼" and ink the edges.
6. Mount the photos to the mat. Adhere mats to the canvas, leaving a 3" gap between the upper and lower pictures.
7. Rub-On the Simply Stated words in the gaps between the photos.
8. Mount a photo on the plaque and secure it to the middle of the canvas using a staple gun.
9. Ink the Hawaii die cut and the wooden letters and mount them above the plaque.

Fabulous beaded trim.

Beads, pearls, and satin create an elegant setting for this truly romantic photograph. Make this canvas for a newlywed couple, or as an anniversary gift.

All You Need Is...

by Emelyn Magpoc

MATERIALS:
- One 14" x 14" Canvas - *Canvas Concepts*
- Light Blue acrylic paint - *Making Memories*
- Patterned paper - *PSX Designs*
- White Satin paper - *K&Company*
- "Love" pillows, Beaded trim - *Michael's* Card Connection
- Pearl strand - *Modern Romance*
- Fiori Font - *2 Peas in a Bucket*
- Adhesives (Glue Dots, foam tape, hot glue gun)
- Blue fiber, heart charm, ribbon, transparency

INSTRUCTIONS:
1. Paint canvas with 2 coats of Light Blue. Let it dry.
2. Cover the canvas with patterned paper. Adhere satin paper.
3. Adhere beaded trim to the back of the photo. Adhere beaded photo to the canvas with foam tape.
4. Print out title on transparency. Use a hot glue gun to adhere the edge of the transparency in place and to attach a pearl strand around the edge of the White satin paper.
5. Attach ribbon and pillows with hot glue.
6. Adhere bow on the corner with Glue Dots. Tie heart charm to ribbon with a Blue fiber.

Fun tags of all kinds strung between beads - terrific!

Capture all aspects of your child's personality in an entertaining layout. Tender, sweet moments and silly photos too, tell a more complete story.

3 Years Old

by Michelle Tornay

MATERIALS:

- One 12" x 36" (or 3-12" x 12") Canvas - *Canvas Concepts*
- Paint (Night Sky, French Blue) – *Plaid* Folk Art
- Paint (Wicker White, Baby Blue) – *DecoArt* Americana
- Numbers patterned paper – *7gypsies*
- Gray cardstock – *Bazzill*
- Stamps – *All Night Media, Hero Arts*
- UTEE clear embossing powder – *Suze Weinberg*
- Ink pads - *Tsukineko* Versamark, StazOn
- Ink – *Nick Bantock*
- Letter stickers – *me & my Big ideas*
- Brads, Star eyelet charm, Round metal tag, Vellum tags – *Making Memories*
- Beads – *Westrim Crafts*
- Ribbon – *Garden Gate Designs*
- Poetry dog tags - *Clare Ultimo*
- Shipping tags (Small, Large), Round metal rimmed tag – *Avery*
- Font (Army Men) – *Chatterbox*
- Font (Evergreen) – *2 Peas in a Bucket*
- Adhesive (Tape) - *3L*
- Wooden "3", photo corners, star hooks, fishing line, stencil, masking tape

INSTRUCTIONS:

1. Use masking tape to separate the areas. Paint a 5" wide stripe on both sides of the canvas with Night Sky. Paint the remainder of the canvas French Blue.
2. Paint the "D" stencil Baby Blue. Adhere the letter stickers below the "D".
3. Paint the wooden 3 with Baby Blue. Paint the star hooks and brads with Wicker White.
4. Run a Black ink pad along the sides of the canvas.
5. Cut 2 strips each of Numbers paper 2" x 12" and 2⅞" x 5". Cut Gray cardstock: two strips 4¼" x 6" and one strip 4¼" x 10".
6. Ink the edges of all strips and the stencil with Black.
7. Stencil words on Gray cardstock with Black ink.
8. Tape small numbers paper on each end of the canvas. Tape the stenciled Gray cardstock in place. Tape long strips of Numbers paper in place.
9. Mount the wooden "3" in the upper right side of the canvas. Tape the ribbon in place.
10. Mount photos using the photo corners.
11. Mount the star hooks as shown in photo.
12. Tie a 36" piece of fishing line to one star.
13. String beads on the fishing line and tie the different tags to the line using the ribbon.
14. Stamp the vellum tags.
15. Using the Evergreen font, print little sayings on paper and cut the sayings into tags. Punch holes in the top of tags and string them on the line.
16. Paint the Poetry dog tags White. Let dry. Rub tags on the Versamark pad and heat emboss with UTEE. Tie the dog tags to the fishing line.
17. Stamp the metal eyelet and tag with StazOn and tie them to fishing line.
18. After the fishing line is full, tie the loose end to the other star.

Pink and black look elegant together, and provide the perfect setting for these enchanting black and white photos. Display your finished creation on your favorite wall or choose a lovely stand to set off your work of art.

Fancy butterflies and elegant beaded ribbon.

GIRLS ARE LIKE BUTTERFLIES

by Michelle Tornay

MATERIALS:

- Two 12" x 12" (or 1-12" x 24") Canvases - *Canvas Concepts*
- Ballet Pink paint - *Plaid* Folk Art
- Wicker White paint – *DecoArt* Americana
- Black paint - *Crafter's Edition*
- Black Satin paper - *K&Company*
- Transparency - *Hewlett Packard*
- Size 36 Scriptina Font
- Adhesive (Tape) - *3L*
- 9 x 12 inch wooden plaque, 2 wooden butterflies
- Beaded ribbon, photo corners, clear photo tabs, staple gun

INSTRUCTIONS:

1. Paint canvases and plaque Ballet Pink. Let dry.
2. Paint the wooden butterflies Black with Pink and White accents.
3. Staple the 2 canvases together side by side.
4. Tape the satin paper in the middle of the canvas.
5. Tape the beaded ribbon to the canvas on both sides of the satin paper.
6. Center the plaque on the satin paper. Tape in place. Then, turn canvas over and staple thru the back of the canvas to the plaque.
7. Computer print words on transparency.
8. Cut the transparency to fit the plaque.
9. Adhere the transparency to the plaque with clear photo tabs on each corner.
10. Mount a 5" x 7" photo on the plaque.
11. Adhere photos to canvas with photo corners and 3L tape.
12. Tape butterflies in place.

Metal photo corners are fun!   Printing logos are perfect!   Cork tag • Metal Charms • Eyelets

Ashley's favorite time of the year is the Fall. I made this canvas so everyone can share her joy in this happy season.

Fall Favorite

by Krista Fernandez

MATERIALS:

- One 12" x 36" (or 3-12" x 12") canvas - *Canvas Concepts*
- Cape Cod paint - *Delta* Ceramcoat
- Cardstock (Tan, Navy)
- Patterned paper (Soda fountain stripe, Inkwell on Cream words, Large Cream/Inkwell letters, Printing logo) - *Mustard Moon*
- Image Tree Antique alphabet rubber stamps - *EK Success*
- Black ink pad - *Hero Arts*
- Photo corners, Snaps, Leaf eyelet charms, Metal charm alphabet - *Making Memories*
- Book plate - *Li'l Davis*
- Eyelets - *Dritz*
- Walnut ink, cork, fiber, sand paper

INSTRUCTIONS:

1. Paint canvas.
2. Cut 2 pieces of striped paper, 10½" x 11½" and 1½" x 11½". Moisten, crumple, flatten, sand and color with Walnut ink. Adhere to canvas.
3. Mat large photo onto Navy cardstock and printed paper. Attach 2 leaf eyelets. Adhere to striped paper.
4. Cut cork in a tag shape 2¾" x 4¾". Add "fall" letters and metal charms. Add eyelets and thread fiber through. Adhere to canvas. Wrap fiber around the back of the canvas and staple.
5. Mat 4 smaller photos on Tan cardstock and adhere to the canvas. Add metal photo corners. Cut out letters for words.
6. Cut 2 flowers out of cork. Add snaps. Adhere to canvas.
7. Cut out 3 printing logos. Adhere to canvas.
8. Stamp "Ashley" onto cork. Attach to strip of patterned paper. Cover with book plate.

The keys to being children are also the keys to a happy life. Bring the joy of childhood out of your scrapbook and onto your wall with this happy and playful hinged canvas trio.

Terrific metal and vellum keys, cork letters too.

Lovely heart with peak-a-boo and scalloped edge.

Keys to Being Children

by Emelyn Magpoc

MATERIALS:
- One 6", Three 8" Canvases - *Canvas Concepts*
- Wisteria acrylic paint - *DecoArt* Americana
- Mod Podge - *Plaid*
- Vellum Keys Collage paper - *Design Originals*
- Red ink pad - *Rubber Stampede*
- Cork letters, Keyhole & heart - *LazerLetterz.com*
- Metal letters - *K&Company*
- Vintage keys - *Paper Bliss*
- Ribbon - *Offray*
- Adhesive (Diamond Glaze) - *JudiKins*
- Adhesive (Glue Dots)
- Screw eyes, staples

INSTRUCTIONS:
1. Paint canvases with 2 coats of Wisteria.
2. Tear vellum. Staple to canvases.
3. Coat the entire canvas with Mod Podge to seal the paint and papers.
4. Attach the screw eyes as shown. Use ribbon to connect the 4 canvases together.
5. Adhere photos with Glue Dots. Adhere cork products for title and quotes with Diamond Glaze. Ink the title block and heart with Red.
6. Add ribbon to vintage keys and adhere to canvases with Diamond Glaze.

Dewey is our exceptional black lab. He is so gentle and loving, and he is so much a part of our family that he deserves a portrait too. This photograph is one of my favorites.

A bright Red book plate holds the title here. Love the ribbon too!

Ideal zipper pulls an a great touch.

A PET'S LOVE

by Michelle Tornay

MATERIALS:
- One 14" x 14" Canvas - *Canvas Concepts*
- Black paint - *Crafter's Edition*
- Patterned paper, Twill letters - *Carolee's Creations*
- Red cardstock - *Bazzill*
- Ink - *Nick Bantock*
- Ink - *Tsukineko* StazOn
- 2 Wooden flowers, Red book plate - *Li'l Davis*
- Letter stickers - *DoodleBug*
- Zipper pulls ("Woof", "Puppy", "Hydrant") - *Junkitz*
- Ribbon - *Making Memories*
- Playing cards
- Adhesive (Tape) - *3L*
- Adhesive (Scrappy Glue) - *Magic Scraps*
- Adhesive (Glue Dots)
- Safety pins, photo corners, jump rings

INSTRUCTIONS:
1. Paint the canvas Black. Let it dry.
2. Tear a 12" x 12" patterned paper, starting at the right corner and continue to the other side at a small angle.
3. Ink the edges of the patterned paper and a 12" x 12" Red cardstock.
4. Tape the patterned paper to the cardstock.
5. Mount the letter stickers for the title.
6. Glue the wooden flowers on the right hand side of the paper.
7. Affix an 8" x 10" photo with tape and photo corners.
8. Ink the edges of 3 playing cards with StazOn. Attach to the patterned paper with Glue Dots.
9. Tie the ribbon to the book plate. Print journaling to fit inside book plate. Adhere bookplate with journaling to paper with Glue Dots.
10. Ink the zipper pulls with Stazon. Insert a jump ring, and thread them on the ribbon.
11. Tape the ends of the ribbon to the back of the paper.
12. Adhere each zipper pull to the patterned paper using Glue Dots.
13. Insert a safety pin through each twill letter. Attach each letter to the cards using Glue Dots.
14. Adhere cardstock and patterned paper to the middle of the canvas.

A silky stitched label calls this creative piece 'Son'.

Add whimsy with playful wood tiles and a zig-zag stitch.

Colorful truck knobs are just the ticket!

A Son Is...

by Michelle Tornay

MATERIALS:
- One 14" x 14" Canvas - *Canvas Concepts*
- Deep Midnight Blue paint - *DecoArt* Americana
- Mod Podge - *Plaid*
- Patterned paper - *Mustard Moon*
- Blue cardstock - *Bazzill*
- Blue ink pad
- "Son" label - *me & my Big ideas*
- Little wooden letters - *Associate Art Specialists*
- Scrabble tiles - *Hasbro*
- Ribbon - *Offray*
- Adhesive (Tape) - *3L*
- Truck knobs

These photos were so expressive, I couldn't just leave them in a scrapbook. Now this canvas hangs in Daniel's room. The truck drawer knobs were the perfect accent for this project.

INSTRUCTIONS:
1. Drill 3 holes in the canvas 1" above the bottom. Measuring from the left, drill a hole at 1½", at 7", and at 12½".
2. Paint the entire canvas Blue. Let dry.
3. Apply one coat of Mod Podge. Let dry.
4. Mount the truck knobs to the drilled holes.
5. Zig-zag stitch the ribbon to the patterned paper.
6. Tape the patterned paper to the canvas.
7. Cut 3 cardstock mats 4¼" x 6¼".
8. Mount the photos to the mats and sew around each one.
9. Adhere matted photos to the patterned paper.
10. Ink the wooden letters. Tape letters and "son" label in place.

Your Smile

by Suzy West

I found my daughter's favorite doll in a box in the attic, and was inspired to collage this canvas. Now I get a happy memory every time I see it. I'm so glad I didn't leave these things in storage!

MATERIALS:
- One 14" x 14" Canvas - *Canvas Concepts*
- Blue paint
- Pattern paper - *7gypsies*
- Brown ink pad
- Doll
- Letter stickers, Ribbons - *me & my Big ideas*
- Twill letters - *Carolee's Creations*
- Metal letters - *Making Memories*
- Heart stickers - *Pebbles Inc.*
- Adhesive (Scrappy Glue) - *Magic Scraps*
- Adhesive (double-sided tape)
- Silver eyelets, Gray tag

INSTRUCTIONS:
1. Paint the bottom half of the canvas Blue and let it dry. Ink the unpainted edges.
2. Tear paper. Ink the edges.
3. Tape the paper to the canvas.
4. Wrap ribbons around the canvas. Tape ribbon ends to the back of the canvas.
5. Computer print "Love" and "love definitions". Attach "Love" to tag with eyelets. Thread ribbon through tag and wrap around canvas. Adhere tag in place. Adhere "love definition" and heart stickers.
6. Adhere photo in place.
7. Adhere title with Scrappy Glue. Add heart stickers. Tape ribbon across the upper right corner.
8. Use a staple gun to attach the doll directly to the canvas.

Key To My Heart

by Suzy West

Here's a clever way to dress up the average key hook. Choose the most captivating, expressive 8" x 10" photo you have, and have fun making this project.

MATERIALS:
• One 12" x 12" Canvas - *Canvas Concepts*
• Paint - *Delta*
• Pattern Paper - *Chatterbox*
• Cardstock (Yellow, Green)
• Foam Stamps - *Making Memories*
• Brown ink pad
• Metal Letters - *Colorbok*
• Wood Letters - *Li'l Davis*
• Game Letter tiles - *EK Success*
• Letter Stickers - *me & my Big ideas*
• Adhesive (double-sided tape, glue)
• Key hook, keys

INSTRUCTIONS:
1. Paint the canvas. Let it dry.
2. Tear paper. Ink the edges. Tape to canvas.
3. Mat the photo. Tape to canvas. Add triangle shaped paper corners.
4. Screw in the key holder to the bottom of the canvas. (The edges of the canvas have a wood base.)
5. Stamp the word "You" with Yellow paint.
6. Glue down all your embellishments to make your title.
7. Hang your keys on the key holder.

My sister Jacky has a smile that sparkles brighter than starlight. Her personality really shines in this wonderful black and white photograph. Many of her favorite things are symbolized in the embellished coin holder. I hope you have as much fun as I did making a canvas for someone you love.

Star

by Krista Fernandez

MATERIALS:
- One 14" x 14" Canvas - *Canvas Concepts*
- Paint (Silver, Black) - *Plaid*
- Patterned paper (Wordsearch) - *KI Memories*
- Black Satin paper - *K&Company*
- Cardstock (Dark Red, Black)
- Black marker - *Zig* Writer
- Stencil letters - *Ma Vinci*
- Star hook, Decorative corners - *Provo Craft*
- Rhinestones - *Crafting Expressions*
- Charm - *Doodlebug*
- Ribbon - *Offray*
- Punch (Flower, Circle) - *Carl Mfg.*
- Flower eyelets - *Creative Imaginations* Extreme Eyelets
- "Hope" label - *Pebbles Inc.*
- Nature Texture Template - *Fiskars*
- Empressor rolling embossing tool - *Chatterbox*
- Hearts - *Heidi Grace Designs*
- Mini Simply Stated, Black brad, Eyelet alphabet, Star alphabet, Black button, Heart shaped clip, Metal word, Random alphabet charms, Round metal rimmed tag - *Making Memories*
- Red embroidery floss, small binder clip, Silver shamrock charm, coin holder, ticket

INSTRUCTIONS:
1. Paint the lower half of the canvas Silver. Let dry.
2. Adhere an 8½" x 11" Dark Red cardstock to the upper left corner and a 5½" x 11" Black satin paper to the upper right corner of the canvas. Adhere ribbon to cover the seam.
3. Stencil the word "star" using Black paint and add rhinestones.
4. Mat photo on Black cardstock.
5. To create photo corner, tear a piece of Red cardstock. Moisten cardstock with water and emboss it. Let dry. Adhere under lower left corner of photo mat. Set eyelet charm letters and thread embroidery floss around them. Adhere to canvas.
6. Adhere coin holder and fill with various embellishments.
7. Mount star hook and tie ribbon for decoration.
8. Adhere decorative corners.

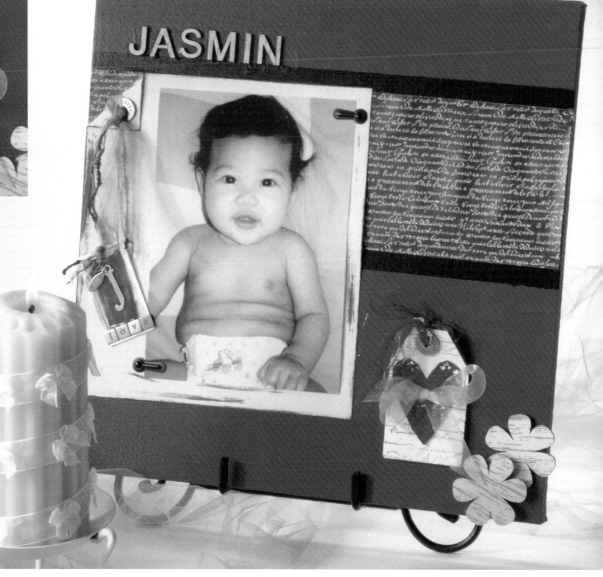

Make a wonderful sweetheart tag to hold your message of love.

Love You, Jasmin! Here's a canvas fit for Valentine's Day. A strong red and black background is softened by the pink mat on this lovely artwork. The accordion fold tag book opens to reveal a message of love.

SWEETHEART

by Emelyn Magpoc

MATERIALS:

- One 14" x 14" Canvas - *Canvas Concepts*
- Acrylic paint (Barn Red, Black) - *Plaid*
- Mod Podge - *Plaid*
- Pink cardstock - *Bazzill*
- Patterned paper, Photo turns - *7gypsies*
- Rubber stamps - *Hero Arts*
- Ink - *Rubber Stampede*
- Wood (Letters, Flowers) - *Li'l Davis*
- Washer words, Metal rimmed tag, Eyelet letter, Alpha charms- *Making Memories*
- Red eyelets - *Doodlebug*
- Brads - *Creative Impressions*
- Fibers - *Maya Road*
- Ribbon - *Offray*
- Adhesive (Diamond Glaze) - *JudiKins*
- Adhesive (Pop Dots, Glue Dots)
- Wire, stencil, masking tape

INSTRUCTIONS:

1. Paint canvas with 2 coats of Red. Let dry.
2. Using masking tape as guides, paint Black lines.
3. Trim paper to fit between Black lines. Adhere to canvas. Coat the entire canvas with Mod Podge to seal the paint.
4. Trim Pink cardstock larger than the photo. Adhere photo and place photo turns in opposite corners. Use brads to secure photo turns. Fold top left corner of the cardstock. Attach washer word with Glue Dots in the folded corner and tie fibers and ribbon.
5. Paint the tag Red. Attach eyelet letter and year tag with wire. Use Glue Dots to adhere Alpha Charms. Attach tag at the other end of the fibers and ribbon. Adhere to cardstock.
6. Make tag booklet: Cut cardstock 3½" x 9". Accordion fold in 4 sections. Cut angles at the top to form a tag shape. Stamp script on the front cover and insides of the tag booklet. Attach washer words for tag tops and attach fibers for each section of the tag. Stencil "LOVE" with acrylic paint. Paint handmade heart Red and attach to front of tag booklet.
7. Attach eyelets directly to the canvas on each side of the tag booklet. Adhere tag booklet to canvas. Thread ribbon through eyelets and tie a bow to hold tag booklet closed.
8. Adhere 1 wooden flower directly to the canvas. Use Pop Dots on the other flower to create dimension. Adhere wooden letters with Diamond Glaze.

I cherish the wonderful relationship I have with my sister. Let someone you love know how you feel with this great canvas.

Sisters Always

by Krista Fernandez

MATERIALS:

- Two 14" x 14" Canvases - *Canvas Concepts*
- Pink Blush paint, Mod Podge - *Plaid*
- Patterned paper (Black Blossom, Lipstick Capri Stripe) - *KI Memories*
- Patterned paper (Black Splatter, Black Dots, Black Gingham) - *Making Memories*
- Cardstock (Black, Pink) - *Bazzill*
- Dawn Houser stamp - *Inkadinkado*
- Playful Heart alphabet rubber stamps - *Ma Vinci*
- Black ink pad - *Hero Arts*
- Black marker - *Zig* Writer
- Eyelets, Shaped clips, Metal eyelet phrases, Buttons, Mini Simply Stated - *Making Memories*
- Woven label - *me & my Big ideas*
- Buttons - *Dress It Up*
- Aluminum - *Art Emboss*
- Drapery ring clips - *Loft Umbra*
- Li'l Trinkets, Bubble type - *Li'l Davis*
- My Type concho brad alphabet - *Colorbok*
- Flower wall pegs - *Target Flowers Etc Collection* Restore and Restyle Kids
- Transparency - *7gypsies*
- Ribbon (Fruit punch gingham, Black satin, sheer Pink) - *Offray*
- Heart metal charm, Word brad - *JoAnne Scrap Essentials*
- Silver brad, star brad, fibers, tiny tags, cording, jump ring, staple gun

INSTRUCTIONS:

1. Staple canvases together in the back.
2. Paint canvases Pink. Coat with Mod Podge for glossy finish.
3. Diagonally tear a 12" x 12" sheet of Black Blossom paper in half. Adhere to opposite corners of the canvas.
4. Adhere transparency to right side of the canvas using a brad and adhesive which will be hidden under the photo.
5. Adhere a matted photo to the transparency. Attach 2 strips of Black Splatter paper to the right side of the photo and attach buttons.
6. Cut Black cardstock 7¼" x 8½". Trim and mount 3 smaller photos onto Black cardstock. Mat onto Gingham paper. Mat again onto Pink cardstock. Ink edges. Mat again on Black cardstock. Adhere to canvas.
7. Title box: Stamp the word "sisters" onto a Light Pink cardstock. Attach letters. Handwrite the word "the". Wrap 2 fibers around the bottom. Cut a heart out of aluminum and dry emboss design using a stylus. Adhere to title block. Glue title box in place.
8. Cut 2 mats out of Capri Stripe paper. Stamp with collage image. Mat the photos.
9. Cut a piece of Black Splatter paper. Moisten, crumple and flatten. Adhere to canvas. Adhere photo. Attach metal word.
10. Attach flower wood pegs by screwing in through the back of the canvas. Tie on cording.
11. "laugh often" Tag: Tear Capri Stripe paper and stamp collage image onto it. Attach photo. Attach woven title using a shaped paper clip. Add buttons for accent.
12. "forever friends" Tag: Cut, moisten, crumple and flatten a piece of Black Splatter paper. Adhere a strip of Pink cardstock. Mat photo and adhere to tag. Using eyelets, thread ribbon, tie. Add a metal photo corner and eyelet phrase.
13. "memories" Tag: Mount photo onto transparency and wrap trim around bottom of photo. Adhere to Capri Stripe paper. Attach jump rings to tiny tags. Attach to eyelets. Attach "laugh" tiny tag with brad.
14. Using drapery clips, hang tags from cording, tie ribbon for security.

Grace your wall with a timeless antique photograph presented in popular nostalgic collage. Aging the elements to make this project is fun and easy, and the skill transfers to so many other projects, you will be glad you did this one first!

Timeless

by Michelle Tornay

MATERIALS:
- One 14" x 14" Canvas - *Canvas Concepts*
- Linen paint - *Plaid* Folk Art
- Patterned paper - *Carolee's Creations*
- Brown cardstock - *Bazzill*
- Stamps - *Ma Vinci*
- Brown ink pad - *Nick Bantock*
- Fabric - *Junkitz*
- Tags, "Time" label - *Pebbles* Real Life
- School Books paper - *Design Originals*
- Clock face, Twill (Remember, Journey) - *7gypsies*
- Key, Clock hands - *Limited Editions*
- Button stickers - *K&Company*
- Fiber - *On the Fringe*
- Gingham ribbon - *Garden Gate Designs*
- Cork label - *Laser Letterz*
- Typewriter key stickers - *Li'l Davis*
- Washer word - *Making Memories*
- Adhesive (Tape) - *3L*
- Adhesive (Scrappy Glue) - *Magic Scraps*
- Photo corners, staples, burlap ribbon, cabinet handle

INSTRUCTIONS:
1. Paint the canvas with Linen paint. Let it dry.
2. Glue the fabric to the upper left side of the canvas.
3. Cut a strip of Brown cardstock 2" x 14". Glue to the bottom of the canvas.
4. Ink and glue the striped paper on the upper right side of the canvas.
5. Print "Timeless" on a piece of patterned paper and ink the edges. Glue in place.
6. Glue the burlap ribbon over the seam between the Brown cardstock and striped paper.
7. Drill 1 hole in the upper left hand side of the canvas. Use the hole to screw the handle on to the canvas.
8. Mount the typewriter keys to the bottom left hand side of the canvas.
9. Stamp the cork label with Brown ink.
10. Attach a brad to both sides of the cork label and mount it on top of the burlap ribbon.
11. Tie the washer word and the key to the smaller tag with a fiber.
12. Adhere the small "time" label to the tag.
13. Tie the tag to the cabinet handle.

Stamped labels work great for recording time.

14. Ink 2 large tags and twill ribbons with Brown.
15. Staple twill ribbon word to each tag. Add button stickers to "remember" tag. Add clock face and hands to "journey" tag. Add gingham ribbon to both tags. Adhere tags to canvas.
16. Cut out 2 books from School Books paper. Glue in place.
17. Adhere photo and photo corners.

I Can Spell My Name

by Emelyn Magpoc

When Jordan learned to spell his name, he was so proud, and you can tell from the photos! I was proud too, as everyone can tell from this canvas. Jordan wrote his name himself - what a wonderful moment to capture!

MATERIALS:
- One 14" x 14" Canvas - *Canvas Concepts*
- Chalkboard paint - *Krylon*
- Patterned papers - *Mustard Moon*
- Wooden blocks, chalk, twine

INSTRUCTIONS:
1. Spray canvas with 2 coats of chalkboard paint. Let dry.
2. Adhere wooden blocks at the top of the canvas.
3. Arrange patterned paper to create background.
4. Tie chalk with twine and wrap around wooden block.

Every now and then, you come across a piece of art that touches you so deeply you are compelled to display it where it can be appreciated every day. This project is one of those pieces. Carefully selected photos convey a powerful message of unconditional love in this black and white grouping. The subtle green and brown setting focuses attention on these beautifully preserved photographs.

Pure Love

by Michelle Tornay

MATERIALS:
- Three 8" x 8" Canvases - *Canvas Concepts*
- Sage Green acrylic paint
- Patterned paper - *Chatterbox*
- Cardstock - *Bazzill*
- Ink - *Nick Bantock*
- Scrabble letter stickers - *Making Memories*
- Typewriter key stickers - *Nostalgiques*
- Tape measure stickers - *K&Company*
- 2 yards ribbon - *Offray*
- Staples

INSTRUCTIONS:
1. Paint all canvases.
2. Tear and ink 12 strips of 1" x 8" cardstock. Mount one to the top and bottom of each painted canvas. Save the others for the photos.
3. Apply the Scrabble stickers to the top of the first and third canvas.
4. Apply the typewriter key stickers to the top of the middle canvas.
5. Apply the measuring tape stickers to the bottom of each canvas.
6. Cut 3 pieces of striped paper 4⅞" x 8". Cut 3 pieces of solid paper 5" x 8".
7. For all 3 striped papers: Mat the stripe onto the solid. Sew a zig zag stitch along the edge to hold them together. Ink the edges. Glue the 1" x 8" strips to the back of the mats, so part of it sticks out on the top and bottom.
8. Adhere 4" x 6" photos to the mats. Attach to the center of each canvas.
9. Position all 3 canvases on a table, 1" apart. Leaving a 10" tail, start at the top and staple a ribbon along the side of each canvas, traveling along the bottom, and returning up the other side. Leave another 10" tail. Tie the tails in a bow.

You'll absolutely love Scrabble tile stickers!

There's a lot of love in this family, and it shows! Make every day "Love Day" at your house and celebrate the love in your family with this wonderful pair of Valentine canvases.

INSTRUCTIONS:
1. Paint canvas with 2 coats of Red paint.
2. Ink the doilies with Red and Black. Adhere them to the canvases.
3. Adhere letter stickers.
4. Coat the entire canvas with Mod Podge to seal the paint.
5. Adhere photos, acrylic embellishments, metal holder, and heart pillows to canvas.
Instructions for Altered CD:
6. Trim Red patterned paper to the size of the CD.
7. Add music patterned paper.
8. Print vintage angel onto transparency.
9. Adhere title, acrylic hearts, and transparency. Adhere CD to canvas.

Say it with stickers!

LOVE DAY

by Emelyn Magpoc

MATERIALS:
- Two 12" Canvases - *Canvas Concepts*
- Red acrylic paint - *Making Memories*
- Mod Podge - *Plaid*
- Music patterned paper - *7gypsies*
- Red stripe patterned paper - *Heidi Grace*
- Ink (Red, Black) - *Rubber Stampede*
- Acrylic embellishments - *Heidi Grace*
- Letter stickers - *Doodlebug*
- "Crafty" computer font
- Adhesive (Diamond Glaze) - *JudiKins*
- Adhesive (Glue Dots)
- Transparency, CD, metal holder, doilies, heart pillows

Trip to Asia

by Emelyn Magpoc

MATERIALS:
- One 12" x 24" (or 2-12" x 12") Canvas - *Canvas Concepts*
- Copper acrylic paint - *Plaid*
- Oriental papers
- Dragon Coins - *Maya Road*
- Metallic netting, Fibers, Mini dice, Picture pebbles, Oriental good luck sign, Envelope, Tassel ornament - *Scraps-n-more.com*
- Mahjong tiles
- Adhesives (foam tape, hot glue gun)

Do you remember the little shop where we found that coin? This project is going to trigger a different memory every time you look at it. Using memorabilia from your trip will make your canvas just as vibrant and exotic as the experience.

INSTRUCTIONS:
1. Paint canvas with 2 coats of acrylic paint.
2. Arrange Oriental paper and photos as shown.
3. Attach metallic netting.
4. Tie dragon coins to fibers and attach over metallic netting at the top.
5. Attach tassel ornament.
6. Attach Oriental good luck sign with foam tape.
7. Slide Oriental envelopes under the metallic netting on the bottom.
8. Adhere dragon coins on the metallic netting.
9. Adhere picture pebbles, more dragon coins and game tiles as shown.

Remember all those bright, sunny, September days with a festive fall collection of canvases. The photos are as cheery as the sunflowers. This project is easy to do, quick to make, and as much fun as recalling those last days of Autumn.

Lovely Autumn

by Michelle Tornay

MATERIALS:
- Six 6" x 6" Canvases - *Canvas Concepts*
- Burnt Sienna paint – *Delta* Ceramcoat
- Patterned paper – *Petals & Possibilities*
- Brown ink pad
- Gingham ribbon – *Garden Gate Designs*
- 28 screw eyes
- Adhesive (Tape) - *3L*
- Adhesive (Scrappy Glue) - *Magic Scraps*
- 3 silk sunflowers

INSTRUCTIONS:
1. Paint all canvases with at least 2 coats of Burnt Sienna. Let dry.
2. Ink the edges of the canvases with a Brown ink pad.
3. Measure each canvas for screw eyes (1 inch in on both sides, depending on how the canvases are linked together).
4. Screw in all 28 screw eyes.
5. Link the canvases together one at a time and close the screw eyes around each other.
6. Tie pieces of Black gingham ribbon around the screw eyes.
7. Cut 6 patterned paper squares 5" x 5".
8. Ink the edges of the paper with a Brown ink pad.
9. Tape the 5" x 5" pieces of patterned paper on the canvases.
10. Glue the sunflowers on every other canvas.
11. Cut the photos into 4" x 4" squares.
12. Ink the edges of all of the photos with a Brown ink pad.
13. Tape the photos in place.

Mako is the most wonderful dog in the world, and our family loves him so much. I wanted to give his photos a place of significance equal to his own. He is always fetching sticks, so I used one to hang up these canvases.

Wonderful ribbon, just the right touch.

Warm wood tiles spell out your pet's name.

Mako

by Krista Fernandez

MATERIALS:
- Three 6" x 6" Canvases - *Canvas Concepts*
- Mossy Green acrylic paint - *Plaid*
- Texturizing medium - *DecoArt*
- Brown cardstock
- Grosgrain ribbon - *Offray*
- Green plaid ribbon - *Home and More Classic Collections*
- Creative Shapes Alphabet Tiles - *Lara's Crafts*
- Burlap, tree limb, staple gun

INSTRUCTIONS:
1. Mix acrylic paint and texturing medium together on a plate.
2. Paint all 3 canvases Mossy Green. Let dry.
3. Mat photos onto Brown cardstock and then onto burlap. Adhere to the canvases.
4. Attach wooden alphabet tiles to canvas.
5. Staple ribbon to the back of the canvas and loop over tree branch.
6. Tie 3 smaller pieces of ribbon to each of the ribbon loops.

TREASURE RIBBON BOARD

by Krista Fernandez

MATERIALS:
- One 14" x 14" Canvas - *Canvas Concepts*
- Pastel Pink craft paint, Mod Podge - *Plaid*
- Green flower brads, Pink mini snaps, White brads, Simply Stated Rub-Ons, Green square buttons - *Making Memories*
- Pink round buttons - *Junkitz*
- Address alphabet stickers - *Chatterbox*
- Ribbon (Pink gingham, Green, White) - *Offray*
- Ribbon (Green gingham, Pink plaid) - *Michaels Country Home Collections*
- Pink ribbon - *Garden Gate Designs*
- Black round buttons - *Dress It Up*
- Wood alphabet - *Li'l Davis*
- Adhesive (Scrappy Glue) - *Magic Scraps*
- Adhesive (Glue Dots)
- Nails

Treasure the fun and laughter with wonderful photos on this simple to make ribbon board. This happy, feminine setting is perfect if you have little girls. However, if you have boys, it is simple to vary the colors of the paint, buttons and ribbon. Adding some burlap or magic mesh will turn this project into a masculine treasure.

INSTRUCTIONS:
1. Paint canvas with 2 coats of Pink.
2. Attach ribbons on each end with nails.
3. Decorate ribbons with buttons and brads.
4. Cover Pink buttons with alphabet stickers to create title. Adhere buttons with Glue Dots.
5. Glue "FUN" wooden letters in place.
6. Rub on "laughter" and cover with Mod Podge to seal it.
7. Add photos.

Inner Strength

by Suzy West

MATERIALS:
- One 14" x 14" Canvas – *Canvas Concepts*
- Green paint – *Delta*
- Mod Podge - *Plaid*
- Pattern paper – *KI Memories*
- Red cardstock
- Ribbon, Wood letters, Wood flowers – *Li'l Davis*
- Metal photo corners, Bead chain, Metal eyelet, Ribbon – *Making Memories*
- Game Tile letters – *Westrim*
- Letter stickers "Inner" – *Sticker Studio*
- Heart sticker – *Pebbles Inc.*
- Rhinestones – *PSX*
- 3 Red mini brads – *Carolee's Creations*
- 2 yards White satin ribbon – *Offray*
- Adhesive (Scrappy Glue) - *Magic Scraps*
- 1 Black drawer pull, Black marker, transparency sheet

There are many qualities about Angel that I admire. I wanted to express that feeling in a tangible way, so I made this canvas for her.

INSTRUCTIONS:
1. Paint the canvas Green. Let dry.
2. Glue pattern paper to the canvas. Glue Black ribbon to the edge of the paper.
3. Glue the Black drawer pull in place.
4. Add photo to the page. Glue metal corners on the photo.
5. Title: Draw a large letter "S" with a Black marker and cut it out. Print the word Beauty on a transparency sheet. Glue title elements in place.
6. Tag: Cut a small tag from Red cardstock. Add a heart sticker. Cut out the word "passionate" and glue it to the tag. Set eyelet. Write the name on the tag. Attach the bead chain to the tag and handle.
7. Add 3 ribbons to the Black handle. Add a brad to each ribbon.
8. Glue wood flowers in place. Glue rhinestones in place.
9. Cover brads and ribbons on the handle with Mod Podge. Cover Tag with Mod Podge. Let dry.
10. Glue White satin ribbon around the outside edge of the canvas.

The Greatest Gift is Love. This photograph of my children inspired the title of this project. Jordan looks so happy hugging his little sister that I wanted to make this moment part of our holiday decorating.

The Greatest Gift

by Emelyn Magpoc

MATERIALS:
- One 14" & three 6" Canvases - *Canvas Concepts*
- Green acrylic paint - *Making Memories*
- Patterned paper - *PSX Designs*
- Patterned paper - *Mustard Moon*
- Walnut ink
- Adhesive (Scrappy Glue) - *Magic Scraps*
- Gold trim, silk flowers, hooks, ribbon, staple gun

INSTRUCTIONS:
1. Paint canvases with 2 coats of Green.
2. 14" canvas: Cover the whole canvas with patterned paper. Adhere photo. Glue ribbon and flowers in place.
3. Staple all 3 small canvases horizontally with a staple gun. Cover the canvas with patterned paper. Glue Gold trim to outline the Red paper. Glue flowers in place.
4. Title: Tear apart letters from Mustard Moon paper. Dip letters into walnut ink mixture to change White letters to Brown. Ink the edges of each letter. Glue in place.
5. Attach hooks to the bottom of the 14" canvas and the top of the title canvas. Make sure the hooks line up so the canvases hang evenly.

Here's the perfect decoration for your sunroom or garden patio. This canvas presents beautiful foliage every gardener will love. The crystal knobs are perfect for hanging up those garden accents.

Great transparency lettering tops off crackle finish.

Hang small accessories on glass dresser knobs.

FIRST BLOOM

by Michelle Tornay

MATERIALS:
• One 12" x 24" (or 2-12" x 12") Canvas – *Canvas Concepts*
• Eucalyptus paint – *Delta Ceramcoat*
• Wicker White paint – *DecoArt* Americana
• Crackle Medium – *Delta Ceramcoat*
• Patterned paper – *K&Company*
• Brown ink pad – *Nick Bantock*
• One 4 x 6 inch Wooden Frame – *PGM*
• Two 2⅝ x 2⅝ inch Frames – *Tyler's*
• 3 Glass Dresser Knobs – *Provo Craft*
• 2 Distressed Buckets – *Garden Gate Designs*
• 1 Distressed Water Can – *Garden Gate Designs*
• Ribbon – *Offray*
• Silk Flowers

INSTRUCTIONS:
1. Paint canvas and frames with Eucalyptus. Let dry.
2. Dry brush a small amount of White paint on the edges of the canvas.
3. Brush the frames with Crackle Medium.
4. When the Crackle Medium is tacky to the touch, paint the frames with White. Let dry.
5. Adhere a little bouquet of silk flowers and a ribbon to the two smaller frames.
6. Print title on a transparency. Cut out words. Adhere words to the top and bottom of the larger frame.
7. Cut a sheet of 12" x 12" flower paper in half. Age the paper with sandpaper. Ink the edges with Brown. Adhere to the bottom half of the canvas.
8. Drill 3 holes ½" above the bottom of the canvas at 2", 12" and 22" from one end.
9. Screw in the glass dresser knobs. Tie a ribbon to each knob.
10. Adhere a ribbon along the top of the paper on the canvas.
11. Mount the crackled frames on the canvas.
12. Hang the little buckets and watering can on the Glass Dresser knobs.

Crimped cardboard adds dimension and texture.

Star charms tied with ribbon accent the true stars.

There's nothing like the crunch of leaves under your shoes in the Fall. You appreciate the warmth of the sun more, knowing it is about to fade for several months of cold. Take many photos of the family enjoying these times and put them together in a fun fall canvas.

Falling Leaves

by Krista Fernandez

MATERIALS:

- Two 12" x 12" (or 1-12" x 24") Canvases – *Canvas Concepts*
- Pattern paper – *Chatterbox*
- Cardstock (Tan, Rust) – *Bazzill*
- Star eyelet, Star charms, Metal letters – *Making Memories*
- Ribbon – *Offray*
- Cork (1 oval 3½" long, 4 squares 1")
- Adhesive (glue)
- Staple gun, corrugated cardboard

INSTRUCTIONS:

1. Staple canvases together.
2. Cut a strip of Tan cardstock 4¼" x 12", adhere to left side of the canvas.
3. Cover the remaining canvas with Rust cardstock.
4. Cut patterned paper 3½" x 19¾". Glue to the bottom of the canvas.
5. Tie ribbon ends together and add star charms to the knot as in photo. Staple other ends of ribbon to the back of the canvas .
6. Mat photo on Rust cardstock.
7. Unlayer cardboard to show ripples. Glue photo mat to cardboard. Adhere to canvas.
8. Mount 2 photos on Tan cardstock.
9. Cut 2 small slits into a cork oval. Thread ribbon through the slits. Add a star charm. Wrap around photo and mat. Tape ribbon ends to the back of the mat. Adhere to the canvas.
10. Attach metal alphabet charms to cork squares and adhere to canvas.

INSTRUCTIONS:

1. Paint small canvases and wooden plaque with 2 coats of Brown. Paint foam heart Red.

2. Cover large canvas with patterned papers.

3. Tear apart corrugated cardboard to show ripples. Paint cardboard Brown. Ink edges with Gray. Adhere photo over cardboard with foam tape. Attach brads to wooden tags. Hot glue tags in place. Hot glue painted foam heart in place. Add airplane nailhead. Hot glue cardboard to upper left corner of the canvas.

4. 8" canvas: Adhere cut up postcard transparencies with Glue Dots. "Hang" old camera from corner. Secure with hot glue. Ink edges of "memories" definition. Adhere with Glue Dots. Tie fiber to metal word tag and adhere to canvas. Hot glue the 8" canvas to the upper right corner of the large canvas. Staple it in place from the back.

5. 6" canvas: Adhere cut up postcard transparencies with Glue Dots. Adhere bottle cap and page pebble to lower left corner. Tie washer words to fibers and wrap around printed mount. Adhere to canvas. Paint "Passport" charm with Brown to get into the ridges and rub off. Adhere charm to the center of the mount with Glue Dots. Hot glue canvas to the middle left corner of the large canvas. Staple it in place from the back.

6. Plaque: Ink the edges. Adhere photo to the plaque with Glue Dots. Hot glue plaque to the canvas. Turn canvas over and staple to secure.

7. Tickets: Hot glue a piece of corrugated cardboard to the lower right corner. Ink the edges of the ticket coupons and adhere with Glue Dots. Attach airplane and compass nailhead over coupons.

8. Create an original transparency in MS Word Art. Attach to canvas.

Travel journals are interesting to share. Now you can create dramatic art for the wall using your travel memorabilia. With all the wonderful travel papers available, you will really enjoy this collage experience.

Australia

by Emelyn Magpoc

MATERIALS:
- One 6", One 8" and One 24" Canvas - *Canvas Concepts*
- Acrylic paint (Brown, Red, Gray) - *Delta*
- Patterned papers - *Design Originals, PSX*
- Gray ink - *Colorbox* Fluid Chalk
- Printed mount - *Design Originals*
- Page pebble, Ticket coupons, Postcard transparency, Nail heads (Airplane, Compass), Fibers, Brads, - *Scraps-n-more.com*
- Washer words, Passport charm, "Memories" Defined - *Making Memories*
- Metal word tag - *K&Company*
- Bottle cap - *Li'l Davis*
- Travel transparency - *Emelyn Magpoc design*
- Adhesive (Glue Dots, foam tape, hot glue gun)
- Corrugated cardboard, wood plaque, wooden tags, foam heart, old camera, staple gun

"You owe it to yourself to be the best you can possibly be - in baseball and in life." Pete Rose

"I see these pictures of you and I am overwhelmed by the love I feel for you. Watching you play ball and seeing the expression in your face when you hit, caught, or made it home. I will cherish these memories that you have given to me."

INSTRUCTIONS:
1. Paint the canvas Green. Let dry.
2. Cut 3 lattice strips 21¾" long and 2 strips 24" long. Cut 9 strips of Balsa 4" long and 9 strips 2" long.
3. Paint lattice strips and balsa White. Let dry.
4. Cut 17½" x 22½" piece of hardware cloth.
5. Attach bookplate to hardware cloth with brads.
6. Staple hardware cloth in place.
7. Nail lattice strips in place. Drill holes for cabinet knobs and attach.
8. Glue balsa strips in place.
9. Add "score" and number stickers.
10. Adhere photos with glue or Pop Dots.
11. Adhere label stickers in place.
12. Computer print journaling. Layer mats. Add metal letter. Glue in place.
13. Cut softball in half. Glue in place. Glue bat to top of canvas.

BASEBALL

by Suzy West

MATERIALS:
- One 24" x 24" Canvas - *Canvas Concepts*
- Paint (Green, White)
- Cardstock (Red, White)
- Quarter inch hardware cloth
- 1¼" lattice strips
- 54" of Balsa wood ¼" wide
- White ½" finishing nails
- Label Stickers - *Pebbles* Real Life
- Metal Alphabets "B" - *Making Memories*
- Stickers (Score, numbers)
- Plastic softball, bat
- Adhesive (Hot glue, Pop Dots)
- White cabinet knobs, brads, book plate, staple gun

INSTRUCTIONS:

1. Paint the canvas Red. Let dry.
2. Adhere 6" strip of paper to the canvas.
3. Add ribbon along the edge of the paper.
4. Cut hardware cloth 2½" x 12". Attach words with Black mini brads. Glue hardware cloth to the canvas.
5. Computer print letters on Red cardstock. Add metal sticker letters. Cut out tag shapes. Cut out Black tags slightly larger than the Red ones. Glue Red tags to Black tags. Set White eyelets. Add jute and knot. Glue tags to canvas. Staple the ends of the jute to the back of the canvas.
6. Mat photo on paper and Black cardstock. Add photo corners. Set eyelet.
7. Cut a 2½" square of hardware cloth. Cut a 2" square of flower Block Accent. Tape to hardware cloth. String jute through eyelet and tie to hardware cloth. Knot jute.
8. Determine the position of the photo. Before adhering photo to canvas, adhere ribbons and words to the right of the photo so the ends are hidden beneath the photo.
9. Glue photo in place.

Tags attached with jute and embellished with metal sticker letters are balanced by wonderful hardware cloth.

Love Will Keep Us Together

by Suzy West

Red, black, and silver create an elegant environment for this black and white photograph. The elements on this canvas are well balanced. The red color emphasizes the passionate love a couple shares. Make this beautiful artwork for yourself, as a wedding gift, or an anniversary present.

MATERIALS:
- One 14" x 14" Canvas - *Canvas Concepts*
- Red paint
- Pattern paper - *7gypsies*
- Cardstock (Red, Black) - *Bazzill Basics*
- Metal Corners, Ribbon - *Making Memories*
- Block Accents - *KI Memories*
- White eyelets - *Happy Hammer*
- Metal Sticker Letters - *Pressed Petals*
- Adhesive (Tape) - *3L*
- Adhesive (Glue)
- Jute, hardware cloth

Show your team spirit with this mini plaque stamped and decorated with your team's name.

Beautiful Gold wood letters over enlarged and printed transparencies of the team and game.

Small wooden tags are attached to canvas using metal brads just their size.

ND Football

by Emelyn Magpoc

MATERIALS:
- Three 8" Canvases - *Canvas Concepts*
- Gold acrylic paint - *Plaid* Apple Barrel
- Letter stamps - *All Night Media*
- Letter stamps - *PSX*
- Black ink pad - *Tsukineko* StazOn
- Football embellishment - *Provo Craft*
- Brads - *Scraps-n-more.com*
- Adhesive (Scrappy Glue) - *Magic Scraps*
- Adhesive (Glue Dots)
- Transparencies, wooden letters, wooden tags, wooden plaques, staple gun

Go Team! Here's an irresistible canvas for any football fan. Whether it's your alma mater or your favorite pro team, show your team spirit and make this canvas for your family's game room.

INSTRUCTIONS:
1. Staple all 3 canvases together.
2. Use various photos from the actual game. Enlarge them. Print them on transparencies and staple to the canvas.
3. Paint wooden letters, tags, and plaques with Gold.
4. Adhere transparency, football embellishment and photo to wooden plaques.
5. Glue plaques and wood letters to canvas.
6. Attach brads to wooden tags.
7. Stamp letters onto plaque and tags.
8. Adhere tags to canvas with Glue Dots.

It's not just square!

Arranging your canvases in an asymmetrical design makes them more interesting. It keeps the eye moving, and it's more fun to create art that is "outside the box". The color blocking on these canvases also adds to the cheerful tone of this presentation. Finally, if you have never used a transparency for a title before, here's your chance. Use of transparency film allows you to take full advantage of the pattern in your paper.

Count Your Blessings

by Krista Fernandez

MATERIALS:
- One 6" x 6", One 14" x 14", Two 8" x 8" Canvases - *Canvas Concepts*
- Victorian Blue acrylic paint - *DecoArt*
- Patterned paper (Poolside, Poolside Mod Blox, Tags) - *KI Memories*
- Green cardstock
- Metal Rimmed Tags, Metal alphabet charms - *Making Memories*
- Transparency - *Hewlett Packard*
- Adhesive (Tape) - *3L*
- Adhesive (Scrappy Glue) - *Magic Scraps*
- Adhesive (Glue Dots)
- Fiber, staple gun, nails

INSTRUCTIONS:
1. Mask off the bottom 3" of the 14" canvas. Paint the remainder Victorian Blue. Let it dry.
2. Cut Poolside paper 3½" x 12". Tape paper to the bottom left side of the canvas. Add a ¾" strip of Poolside Mod Blox paper.
3. Print title on transparency film. Tape film in place so the tape will be under the other canvases.
4. Adhere large photo to largest canvas.
5. Cover smaller canvases with coordinating patterned paper. Mount photos on cardstock and tape to canvases.
6. Glue KI Memories tag to rectangular metal rim tag frame. Add a round metal letter with a Glue Dot. Thread fibers through tag and wrap around the canvas. Staple fibers to the back of the canvas.
7. Use another KI Memories tag behind a round metal tag frame. Add ribbon. Glue to canvas.
8. Insert a scrap of Mod Blox paper behind a square metal tag frame. Add the KI Memories tag and round metal letter with Glue Dots.
9. Nail the smaller canvases to largest canvas from the back.

LOVE

by Suzy West

MATERIALS:
- Four 12" x 12" Canvases - *Canvas Concepts*
- Paint (Brown, Red) - *Delta*
- Pattern paper - *7gypsies*
- Cardstock (Tan, Chocolate) - *Bazzill Basics*
- Rust Ink
- Walnut Ink
- Letter Stickers, Ribbon,
      Ephemera - *me & my Big ideas*
- Metal Letters - *K&Company*
- Adhesive (double-stick tape, glue)
- Wood letters, silk flowers, fibers

If all you need is love, these canvases fill the bill. Choose colors to match your decor and these canvases will complement any room. You will enjoy the simple construction techniques. Adding your own ephemera allows the project to reflect your personality and makes your art more meaningful.

INSTRUCTIONS:
1. Paint all 4 canvases Brown. Let dry.
2. Paint the wood letters Red. Let dry.
3. Tear the pattern paper and ink the edges. Glue it to the canvas.
4. Tear Chocolate cardstock 7" x 7½".
5. Tear Tan cardstock 6" x 6½". Wash with a light solution of walnut ink. Let dry.
6. Adhere Tan cardstock to Chocolate with brads. Tape to canvas.
7. Adhere wood letters to the cardstock.
8. Add photos, charms, metal letters, fibers and ephemera as desired.